THE RHYTHM, RHYME, AND REASON FOR JESUS CHRIST

AWAKE

INSPIRATIONAL PARABLES

authorHOUSE®

AuthorHouse™
1663 Liberty Drive
Bloomington, IN 47403
www.authorhouse.com
Phone: 1 (800) 839-8640

Published by AuthorHouse 03/19/2016

ISBN: 978-1-5049-8628-1 (sc)
ISBN: 978-1-5049-8629-8 (e)

"BIOGRAPHICAL PAGE"

I was born March 20th 1954 in Fitzgerald, GA. I am the last born of 10 children. My family moved to Miami, FL in 1967, and later I moved to Atlanta, GA in 1975.

"ACKNOWLEDGEMENT"

I owe the idea and encouragement of this book to the FAITH that I have in Jesus Christ. If it wasn't for that, this book probably wouldn't have ever happened. I wanted to and thought it a necessity to leave my family a legacy. I also believe it was a need to put some Biblical Principles and Morals in a form that a reader would be entertained and keeping it real at the same time.

"DEDICATION"

This book is dedicated to my family. My wife, Autherine Timmons, Daughters Octavia Purdue (Jeremiah) and Jera Timmons. To my son Barcardius Bryant. Also dedicated to my brothers Jesse L. Timmons and Willie L. Timmons, my sisters Gladys Cole, Lucille Freeman, Mary Harrison, and Barbara Brown and their families. Last but not least, this book is dedicated to my late parents.

"APPRECIATION"

I would like to express my appreciation and gratitude to AuthorHouse Publishing. Especially Mae Genson, Elijah Guzman, and Edward Ponce for without their patience and dedication, all of this would not have come together. Thank you for being there when and where I needed you. I pray you enjoy this project and it shows you the inspiration that I have reached for.

"I AWAKE"

I awake to a fresh new start
I awake also to a grieving angry heart
I awake to hear the magical sounds of the birds singing
I awake anxiously to see what today will be bringing
I awake to wonder what kind of people I'll meet
I awake to wonder if all will be a dead beat
I awake to hear God's voice to conquer my sorrow
I awake to realize it's my choice to except a better tomorrow
I awake to realize there will be obstacles in my way
I awake also to know that all I have to do is pray
I awake to thrive for God's will
I awake to know that then is when my destiny is beginning to be fulfilled

JERRY TIMMONS

"HOW DO I LOVE THE LORD"

How do I love the lord, I love the lord, when I stop hating my sister and brother
How do I love the lord, I love the lord, when I spread my love to one another
How do I love the lord, I love the lord, when I am on the same accord
How do I love the lord, I love the lord, when I don't gossip about my neighbor
How do I love the lord, I love the lord, when I ask my neighbor does he need a favor
How do I love the lord, I love the lord, when I go to a person in need
How do I love the lord, I love the lord, when I extend a helping hand indeed
How do I love the lord, I love the lord, when I have
mercy on a man that's begging for money
How do I love the lord, I love the lord, when I don't snicker, grin, or think it's funny
How do I love the lord, I love the lord, when I spread God's joy into the atmosphere
How do I love the lord, I love the lord, when I conquer all doubt, confusion, and fear
How do I love the lord, I love the lord, when I bow my knees to pray
How do I love the lord, I love the lord, when I learn how to be obedient and obey
How do I love the lord, I love the lord, when I don't worship any other way
How do I love the lord, I love the lord, when I don't give up the fight
How do I love the lord, I love the lord, when I think to do wrong but I decide to do right
How do I love the lord, I love the lord, when I have a savior to guide my life
How do I love the lord, I love the lord, when I except Jesus Christ

JERRY TIMMONS

"I AM CONFIDENT"

I am confident to take on life's greatest challenges
I am confident to escape without brutal malaise
I am confident to walk in a joyous rhythm
I am confident to walk in to graceful wisdom
I am confident to dream the impossible dream
I am confident to believe that Jesus is the reason I'm redeemed
I am confident to walk in the favor of God
I am confident to know that all I need to do is walk in the labor of God
I am confident to be informed of life's greatest knowledge
I am confident to realize it's never too late to go to learn in some college
I am confident to conquer life's struggles
I am confident to leap over life's discouraging hurdles
I am confident to live by the principles of God
I am confident to know that in me is where it actually start

JERRY TIMMONS

"THE PROMISE"

God gave me life into the world, with that in mind
He also made a promise to me so divine
If I was to make a choice to listen to his voice
Like the ultimate sacrifice Jesus made at the cross
That divine act let the enemy know who the boss was
God promised me in John 3:16
That if I believeth on his son, I will have everlasting life
So when the enemy comes to persuade me, I can quickly say no dice
God promised me that no weapon formed against me will never prosper
God promised me if I would stay on his word, I'll be among true gospel
When the enemy comes in to my life and attempt to make a rattle
God promised me to come in and fight my battle
God promised me to be the savior of my soul
He promised to protect and comfort me as I grow old
God promised not to allow anything in my life that I couldn't bare
He promised me that he would always be there
With all life's obstacles, challenges, and predicaments, that it has to put me in
God promised to love me, in spite of all my sins

JERRY TIMMONS

WHO AM I

I was brought here to America under a master plan
All for the greed and power of the white man
I was told that they changed my African name
And would be beaten and whipped until I was tamed
And if that wasn't enough, I was put out to work in unbearable heat
I was told that if I didn't produce I wouldn't eat
I was stripped of the warm nurturing relationship of my mother
I could never get over the fact that they sold my brother to another
If I was caught with a book that I possibly had read
I would be immediately beaten and put in shackles instead
With the fear of me learning how to become free, or even get bold enough to flee
I wasn't allowed to practice my culture and tradition
I was forced to live a life of insecurity and affliction
I was molded not to trust and respect my own race
He knew that as long as you and I are bickering among each other,
He does not have to confront you face to face
That technique is still in affect up to this day
Believe it or not, we are still governed by the Willie Lynch way
Even though I am not necessarily needed anymore
Which makes me wonder all the more, what's really in store
So who am I to think that the master plan has been changed?
But in all actuality it only has been rearranged.

JERRY TIMMONS

"THANK GOD FOR MY GRANDSON"

I know I went through life, and I stumbled a while
But every time I look in the eyes of a great,
Inspiring young man I say to myself...
OH! THAT'S MY GRANDCHILD!
The more I look at him, the more I see,
The life that was planned for me,
"I was blind, but now I see"
I know that with God there is no "TOO LATE"
I realized it's up to me not to procrastinate.
Thanks for all my grands...
You wouldn't believe how proudly they make me stand,
Thinking of them makes my life so happy,
But not more than to hear them say "I LOVE YOU GRAND PAPPY!"
I've been running the race for a long time with this in mind.
Even though I have dropped the baton,
If anyone would pick it up, I know for sure I can count on my GRANDSON!

JERRY TIMMONS

"THE NEW STOCK MARKET"

There is a new market in existence and it is called incarceration
It's not a southern issue anymore it's all over the nation
To be enslaved in this day and time is to go to jail
Unfortunately that's just the beginning of your living hell
I've never understood a particular law,
Stating, you are innocent until proven guilty in a court of law
Which makes me wonder to suspect a flaw
If I am innocent before going to court, why do I have to go to jail?
Until my rights are upheld
Getting convicted for a felony is not always saying that you are guilty
The flip side is when you get released an employer will not
hire you and looks at you as if you were filthy
By being convicted puts you in a perpetuated life style
Every time that you sit down in front of an employer,
You are again put on trial
Man was not made to be put in a cage
It's enough horror to put you in a terrible rage
It defies the law of God, once you are incarcerated your
rights are taken, and things are made very hard
I am a firm believer of the bible, Jesus died for our life's revival
Quote me if I am wrong, Jesus had to be scrutinized with every sin,
That man could be confronted with on this earth, he knew what his destiny was at birth
Jesus never was put in jail
He had another technique to win our rights from hell
You are a commodity when you are incarcerated
Just like the slave market, you are waiting to be traded

JERRY TIMMONS

OPEN YOUR MIND AND READ

A closed mouth can't get fed
And in return a closed mind hinders you from getting ahead
Open your mind and read all you can read
It inspires you to actually succeed
When you want to know the difference between a cop and a crook
Pick up some literature or read a book
I was taught that knowledge is power at any given hour
Reading is part of being educated
Read your history and find out when slavery was emancipated
So read and get knowledge and no one can ever take it away
You'll find it to be useful until your dying day
Opening up your mind allows a lifetime of treasures to be revealed
It can show you how the mind body and soul can be healed
Not reading fluently and collectively puts you under certain restrictions
Who wants to live a life style that everyone has already summed up their predictions

JERRY TIMMONS

"THE ART OF THE MIND"

The mind can be a simple instrument, or it can be very complicated
If you are not careful, your thoughts could have you like a game of chess, check mated
The mind can take you back in time, or it can take you into the future
It can even allow you to face the present
Your thoughts can make your heart joyful and content
If negativity flows, the mind can put you in depression
Thinking positive thoughts has been proven to be a divine lesson
The mind can put you in doubt, or it can give you enough
hope to have something to shout about
A thought not worth sharing is a thought not worth thinking
It's like polluted water that's not worth drinking
Foolish thinking is like cancer to the brain
If not careful, it can drive you insane
Make sure your thinking has a positive impact
Remember this, so what a man thinketh, so is he
Has been proven to be a true fact

JERRY TIMMONS

WHAT ROAD ARE YOU ON?

Are you on the path of the rough and narrow
Just keep the faith, and keep your eye on the sparrow
Are you going down a road that's hard for you to forgive?
Don't forget God forgave you and I
It's just not a Godly way to live
Are you going down a road that makes you hesitate?
Just remember, don't wait too late, you might miss the heavenly gate
Are you going down a road where you see and talk to unwanted voices?
The devil does not want you to know you have choices
Are you going down a road where you are tired of being used and abused?
Some day you have to come to reality and realize
that kind of behavior can't be excused
Are you going down a road that's lacking trustworthiness?
It's plain and simple honesty that will help you pass the test
Are you going down a road of financial hardship?
Don't stop sowing seeds, eventually you will become financially equipped
Are you going down a road, where there seems to be no return
Repent, because in hell is where you will indefinitely burn
Are you going down the road of making bad decisions?
Kneel on your knees and pray, and hold on to the vision

JERRY TIMMONS

"THE ESSENCE OF TIME"

Time is important to any and every breathing thing on earth
Time even brings on birth
Time will heal all wounds
Without it all of mankind is doomed
Maybe my time does not mean anything to you
But it means everything to me
Time is what brought everything to be
Without the respect of one another's time
Definitely it would keep a lot of us in a bind
Without the motion of time being exerted
There would be no need to be convergent
Which means coming to a common point in time is not necessary
Which would make man the more contrary
Time allows us to convey with one another
It's a frightening thought knowing that you can't
communicate with your sister or brother
Time creates another day to get under way
Without time everything would be under suspended animation
There would be a devastating limit to God's creation

JERRY TIMMONS

"REMEMBER ME"

Remember me oh lord of glory
Remember oh lord, when I tell my sinful story
Remember me oh lord, of my selfish ways
Remember me oh lord, of all the praying days
Remember me oh lord and savior
Remember me oh lord, when times of blessings and favour
Remember me oh lord, when I judged my brother
Remember me oh lord, when I shared my joy to one another
Remember me oh lord, at the time of my mischievous adolescent stage
Remember me oh lord, I was just going through a growing phase
Remember me oh lord, of my warped thinking when deciding
Remember oh lord, I know it was your will and grace that was guiding
Remember me oh lord, when I was doubtful to my self
Remember me oh lord, when I encouraged everyone else
Remember me oh lord, if my life hasn't been based on your expectations for you
Remember me oh lord, it was my faith that brought me through
Remember me oh lord, when I was full of disgust and confusion
Remember me oh lord, when I waited on your conclusion
Remember me oh lord, when I leave this forsaken place
Remember me oh lord, with your AMAZING GRACE

JERRY TIMMONS

"HEAR NO EVIL, SEE NO EVIL, SPEAK NO EVIL"

What is a form of brainwashing?
When Satan enticed Eve to pick from the forbidden tree,
He had her thinking, his way is the way it should be
Faith cometh by hearing and hearing by the word of God
But the change starts in your heart
Don't allow your eyes and hand to make you sin
Remember in the heart is where it begins
Misconceptions of the word is a form of brainwashing
Even if it's conceived by one's self
Or forced upon by someone else
God made us with five senses
If one is contaminated, it defies the other
It can also affect your sister or brother
Matthew 15:19 says, for out of the heart proceeds evil thoughts
Everything starts in your heart
In order to change a person's mind, you have to change the way they feel
Trust me my brother, don't lean on your own will
Speaking negative and evil thoughts is a path to condemn man
So speak to your heart my friend to develop a better plan

JERRY TIMMONS

"THE ASSIGNMENT"

WHAT IS YOUR ASSIGNMENT?
DO YOU HAVE AN ASSIGNMENT?

As living beings we all share at least one thing in
common, as human beings and that's life
But unfortunately as individuals, we limit our abilities when we
pick and choose to what we are willing to sacrifice
Since our birth you and I were given an assignment to accomplish here on earth
If you and I do not identify, recognize, or complete our
assignment, our lives aren't fulfilled with its total worth
That assignment was ordained from the heavens above
With the sincere design of God's love
If the enemy's mission is to steal, kill, and destroy
Our mission should be the opposite, to heal, fulfill, and spread joy
Your assignment maybe an elder, deacon, or pastor
Or, it may be to usher, and greet people at the door, it really doesn't matter
All of it will coincide with God's glorification for his kingdom's manifestation
We all are thriving for one mission under God's vision
To demolish all doubt and prepare for his provision that's made by all of his decisions
To be yearning for his word that is so desperately needed to be heard
Jesus died for us on the cross before then, mankind was pretty much lost
So I ask, are you going to be part of that crowd
Or, are you going to acknowledge your assignment to let God's mission be allowed
Along our journey we should have Godly desires and needs
With the expectancy for God's will to succeed.

JERRY TIMMONS

"TRUE FAITH"

True faith is not determined on how much faith you possess
It is determined on what in God's word you are willing to caress
Some people believe in cars and some believe in wars
Some people even believe in the figuration of the stars
God's word is what you absolutely need to build your foundation of belief
It's then when your faith will begin to increase
The bible says whosoever believeth on the son will have everlasting life
With that being said, I pity the fool who would still want to roll the dice
Knowing and having faith in too much of the wrong things, will create doubt and fear
Meditating on God's word will keep it plain and clear
Just knowing the verse (John 3:16) and believing it,
gives you the faith of a mustard seed
It equips you with enough faith the devil can't impede
Don't get me wrong, I am not saying don't have a lot of faith
Having it on the wrong things is a shameful waste
Don't build your faith to your own taste and delight
Because you could be living a life of sin and thinking that it is right
Build with the intent to be strong with God's armor of defense
So when the enemy appears he will quickly return to once he whence

JERRY TIMMONS

"PATIENCE"

WHAT IS PATIENCE?

Patience is the quality of endurance without complaint
It also keeps your emotions under restraint
Patience is also the exercise of perseverance being sustained
It will help your dignity to be maintained
It will also help steer your life on a steady course
It will even prevent you from being easily coerced
Patience is a virtue meditate on God's word day and night
You'll find it to be a divine delight
It will pull you through hasty decision making
It will allow you time to see if you are real or faking
Remember the story of the tortoise and the hare
The hare didn't leave too much room for the tortoise to dare
It is a demonstration of what patience is all about
But after the contest was over, the hare did not have the opportunity to jump and shout
Patience is the spiritual discipline for your soul
Patience is one technique that will help you grow old
Patience is wisdom's first cousin
So remember my friend, have "PATIENCE"
To allow wisdom to seek in

JERRY TIMMONS

"THE SEED OF LIFE"

Reaping what you sow is a divine principle
Therefore, if you don't sow anything, you don't expect for anything to grow
You basically will stop all your blessings from the normal flow
To plant a seed of faith, will build yourself esteem
That particular seed can fulfill your dream
You will have confidence in the word of God
Planting a seed of faith will put you and your lord and savior on the same accord
There will be times when evil and satanic persuasion will try to take over your thought
Feed your mind with the living word and bring it to a halt
Don't let the seed of greed succeed
The bible says in Proverbs 30:15, greed has two daughters
Waiting to take you to the slaughter
Ironically their names are the same
"More and More"
Always keeping you in amazement of what's in store
No matter how much they seem to get, by means of persuasion
The word "enough" will never be met to the occasion
You don't have to embrace your child with the seed of stupidity
It will try to consume them naturally
So plant the seed of faith into a child's heart
For the sake of God he will never depart

JERRY TIMMONS

"THE BROTHERHOOD OF CHRIST"

WHAT IS BROTHERHOOD?

Brotherhood: Is one that is related to one another for a particular purpose
Brotherhood brings us together, like birds of a feather
It forms a relationship of brotherly love
It showers a divine connection from above
Have you ever asked yourself, am I my brother's keeper?
And realize that you have been your brother's deceiver
The first epistle of John 1:6 says, if we say that we have
fellowship with him and walk in darkness
We lie and do not practice the truth
So love and respect one another to form a truce
As brothers of Christ, we are the echoers of the universe
The words of life is universal
When the words of life rings into the heavens, there is always hope for mankind
You can rest assure we are on the main life line
Brotherhood is truly a divine technique
If you are lonely and need companionship
I suggest brotherhood, is what you should seek
Satan wants you to be alone and lonely
Just to think of his devilish deeds only
Remember there is strength in numbers, don't allow separation to put us under
We have to set a path for our youth, we have to make sure they get the truth
We are the trail blazers to overcome
To conquer all the hell raisers against God's kingdom

JERRY TIMMONS

"THE PROCLAMATION AND DECLARATION OF JESUS CHRIST"

Jesus was sent to us to proclaim God's kingdom
Because, before then mankind was doomed
God's rights was restored and revised
Wake up God's people and recognize
Satan had man's life style in such a knot
We were hell bound under a devilish plot
When Jesus died on Calvary he declared and demanded all power over hell
He also confiscated the keys as well
God is so awesome that he sent his only begotten son to protect his kingdom
He came to teach us passion and peace
With the intention of more followers to increase
If all of us could learn from this unselfish act
Our salvation would surely be in tact
According to God's will man was out of line
We were definitely in need of something truly divine
In spite of all the torcher and humiliation that Jesus was put through,
He was still compassionate enough to ask his father,
"Forgive them for they know not what they do"
For the sake of mankind as a whole
By announcing those words, God declared and proclaimed the rights to our souls

JERRY TIMMONS

"LISTEN"

Listening is the process of acquiring knowledge
Listen and enroll in someone's college
Listen and absorb all you can
Listening can equip you to conquer all life's demands
Listen and open your ears
Listening can erase all doubt and fears
Listening builds your confidence
Listening builds an attitude to confront life's consequences
Listening strengthens your faith
Faith cometh by hearing and hearing the word of God
So listen to hear what your heart has to say
It may very well reveal a better way
Listening builds character
Even if it's respect you are after
Listening will help maintain your dignity
Listening will prepare you for your enemy
Listening can bring you comfort today and tomorrow
Listening can avoid you from all kinds of sorrow
Listening can teach you how to correct others
Listening can direct you how to respect your brother
Listening more and talking less will put your skills to an ultimate test
Listening will put your life on an amazing quest
Listen, but pick and choose the good from the bad
Be careful about listening to fools, you might find out you've been had

JERRY TIMMONS

THE IMPORTANCE OF EDUCATION

Elevate (Elevate yourself to a moral and intellectual level)

Dedication (Dedicate yourself to learn all you can)

Understanding (Understand what you study)

Calculating (Be calculating to solve problems)

Aspire (To have a desire to be better)

Training (Willingness to be trainable)

Inspiring (Be able to inspire someone with your intellect)

Observant (Being Observant to absorb all the knowledge you can)

Necessary (Education is definitely necessary to function in this society)

Jerry Timmons

"LISTEN"

Learn (willing to acquire knowledge)
Investigate (capable of searching for important information)
Separate (determine the good from the bad)
Taught (when you listen you are teachable)
Examine (you are able to be put to test)
Negotiate (the ability to agree and disagree)

"LISTENING CAN BE A DELIGHTFUL TREAT FOR YOUR EARS"

JERRY TIMMONS

GOD IS

(ALMIGHTY GOD)

ALFA AND OMEGA (He is the beginning and the end)

LOVING (His passion for us is ever lasting)

MASTER (Ruler over the universe)

INSPIRATIONAL (His word keeps us inspired)

GRACE (We are saved)

HEALING (By his stripes, we are healed)

TRUTH (Gods word is the truth and the light)

YOKELESS (There are no strings attached)

Good (He is good all the time)

Order (There is always order for his will)

Destiny (He wants you in his kingdom)

HE IS EVERYTHING YOU'LL EVER NEED

JERRY TIMMONS

SAVED BY GOD'S GRACE

SALVATION (our salvation was bought and paid for)

AFTER LIFE (we then are judged)

VICTORY (God claims all glory)

ETERNITY (our spirit lives forever)

DELIVERANCE (we are delivered from the condemnation of sin)

JERRY TIMMONS

"THE GREAT I AM"

AM (Al-Mighty)
I AM the answer to all your problems, that seems so hard to solve
Just stay on my word and in time they will be resolved
I AM kind, seek compassion and you shall find
I AM a jealous God, be no other God before me
Stand on my word and I will never forsake thee
I AM a loving God, I am peace
Practicing this causes faith to increase
I AM caring, if it's comfort you are sharing
I AM assurance for your salvation
I AM there for all creations
I AM bold, I even have the audacity to comfort your soul
I AM history's mysteries, I am also the reason for all victories
I AM the now, I am also the then
I AM always with you to the bitter end
With this in mind with all due regard
"I AM THAT I AM, THE ALMIGHT GOD"

JERRY TIMMONS

IN GOD WE TRUST

WHAT IS TRUST (confidence in a person or thing?)
Who or what do you have your most trust in?
Is it your money or is it a friend
Or is it that conniving looking fellow with the mischievous grin
Be careful in trusting on the things you've heard
Especially if it does not coincide with God's word
Our country was and still is built on that phrase
It's very important to put your trust in God in these evil and perilous days
There's one thing for sure that you can put your trust in is
Knowing that if you trust in worldly things
You can rest assured that lots of confusion and disappointment is what it will bring
Be careful about trusting that feeling from the gut
You might find out that you are in an awful rut
Who can you trust? SYLVIA, SARA, or SUE
Or the guy over there that will lie to you
The bible says don't put your faith and trust in man
Most likely he has his own plan
You might find yourself getting disgusted
Finding out that people can't be trusted
So don't allow your trust to get you caught up in a spider's lure
Always put your trust in God's word and his love
It will surely keep you faithful and secure

JERRY TIMMONS

"THE SHIELD"

The shield is absolutely the abundance of God's love
Shining from the heavens above
Penetrating to our souls to be healed
The shield is staying on his word, and in time more will be revealed
The shield is to keep hope alive
With it mankind will be surely to survive
The shield is the faith within
Without it, you don't know if there is a beginning or an end
The shield is favor
It's the love of God that you savor
The shield is to make the right choice
The shield is to listen for his voice
The shield is being grateful of your blessings
Teach it to your sister and brother
It will be proven to be valuable lessons
The shield is to spread joy to the people,
And in return it will create a faith and brotherhood greater than any steeple
The shield is meditating on his word day and night
The shield has already won the fight
The shield is God's grace for the human race
The shield protects you from all your calamities of pass life
The shield even protects you from future strife
The shield has already fought all battles and WON
THANK GOD FOR HIS SON!

JERRY TIMMONS

Printed in the United States
By Bookmasters